PRAISE

What a relief as a mom to find a book on true beauty that I *know* my daughters will love! Dannah's funny examples and BFF-tone will make this an easy read for your tween. It will equip you to have conversations, not confrontations, about hot topics like mini-skirts. Don't let culture dictate what is beautiful to your daughters. Have them read Dannah's book instead.
ARLENE PELLICANE, speaker and author of *31 Days to Becoming a Happy Mom*

Dannah Gresh has always captured the heart and attention of my four daughters and me. Now with *True Girl: Discover the Secrets of True Beauty* she does it again by showing girls that true beauty is based on a lifestyle and not their outfits! This resource speaks the language of younger girls, reaches their hearts, and helps them to understand a truth that will impact their future.
WYNTER PITTS, author of *Hello Stars* and *You're God's Girl: A Devotion for Tweens*

PRAISE FOR THE *True Girl* ministry

I wish *True Girl* had been available when my daughter was moving through her teens.
DR. JAMES DOBSON, bestselling author and host, *FamilyTalk*

As I raise my children, I am grateful for someone like Dannah who is helping me as a parent navigate in a challenging and rapidly changing world.
MATT MARKINS, VP, *Awana*

Discover the
Secrets
of True Beauty

BY DANNAH GRESH

MOODY PUBLISHERS

CHICAGO

©2017 by
DANNAH GRESH

Unless otherwise indicated, Scripture quotations are from *The Holy Bible, English Standard Version.* Copyright © 2000, 2001 by Crossway Bibles, a division of Good News Publishers. Used by permission. All rights reserved.

Scripture quotations marked NIV are taken from the *New International Version®.* NIV®. Copyright © 1973, 1978, 1984, 2011 by International Bible Society. Used by permission of Zondervan Publishing House. All rights reserved.

Scripture quotations marked NLT are taken from the *Holy Bible, New Living Translation,* copyright ©1996, 2004, 2007, 2013, 2015 by Tyndale House Foundation. Used by permission of Tyndale House Publishers, Inc., Carol Stream, Illinois 60188. All rights reserved.

Scripture quotations marked TLB are taken from *The Living Bible* copyright © 1971. Used by permission of Tyndale House Publishers, Inc., Wheaton, Illinois 60189. All rights reserved.

Emphasis in Scripture has been added.

All websites and phone numbers listed herein are accurate at the time of publication but may change in the future or cease to exist. The listing of website references and resources does not imply publisher endorsement of the site's entire contents. Groups and organizations are listed for informational purposes, and listing does not imply publisher endorsement of their activities.

Edited by Cheryl Molin
Author photo: Steve Smith
Cover and interior design, illustrations of girls by Julia Ryan [www.DesignByJulia.com]
Printed by Versa Press in East Peoria, IL, June 2019

Library of Congress Cataloging-in-Publication Data

Names: Gresh, Dannah, 1967- author.
Title: True girl : discover the secrets of true beauty / by Dannah Gresh.
Description: Chicago : Moody Publishers, 2017. | Includes bibliographical references.
Identifiers: LCCN 2017025832 (print) | LCCN 2017032656 (ebook) | ISBN 9780802495471 (ebook) | ISBN 9780802417350 (print)
Subjects: LCSH: Preteen girls--Conduct of life--Juvenile literature. | Preteen girls--Religious life--Juvenile literature. | Modesty--Religious aspects--Christianity--Juvenile literature. | Clothing and dress--Religious aspects--Christianity--Juvenile literature. | Body image in girls--Religious aspects--Christianity--Juvenile literature.
Classification: LCC BJ1651 (ebook) | LCC BJ1651 .G74 2017 (print) | DDC 248.8/33--dc23
LC record available at https://lccn.loc.gov/2017025832

ISBN: 978-0-8024-1971-2

We hope you enjoy this book from Moody Publishers. Our goal is to provide high-quality, thought-provoking books and products that connect truth to your real needs and challenges. For more information on other books and products written and produced from a biblical perspective, go to www.moodypublishers.com or write to:

Moody Publishers
820 N. LaSalle Boulevard
Chicago, IL 60610

1 3 5 7 9 10 8 6 4 2

Printed in the United States of America

Contents

Thanks . . .

First of all, thanks to all the True Girl moms who are concerned about how this world is making their girls grow up too fast and who want to join me on a mission to keep the little in their girl. This all started with six moms in a classroom at my childhood church. And now we're hundreds of thousands of moms strong across the United States, Canada, and the Dominican Republic, with a smattering of moms from other nations jumping on board.

Next, I'd like to thank two really instrumental dads, my husband, Bob Gresh, and my first publisher, Greg Thornton of Moody Publishers, who initially saw the need for a book on true beauty. I am pretty sure it was love for their daughters that made this topic important to them. I wrote such a book for teenagers in 2002, which continues to be a bestseller. And now we finally have *True Girl* for tweens, and these two giants among men are still leading with good ideas and encouragement.

Some practical gratitude goes to Jose Pablo and Charo Michelen de Pablo and their daughter, Sharin Pablo de Roca, for giving me their cozy home nestled in the palm trees, where I wrote this book. To be honest, I was stuck until I heard birds singing from those trees, and there the Spirit of God hushed my spirit enough to begin to hear how this book should be formed. I can't thank you enough.

I'm especially grateful for my new friend Judy Dunagan, my editor at Moody Publishers, because she has a great understanding of why this book matters. And Paul Santhouse, whom I have watched pick up the mantle of leadership at Moody with integrity, excellence, and love. It has been a joy to work with editor Cheryl Molin again.

And finally to my delightful team, which always lifts more for me during a writing deadline. Aaron Burrell, our faithful friend and ministry manager, who has brought order and peace to our team; Eileen King, who has been serving Jesus alongside me for more than a decade; Ashley Munn, whose energy, creativity, and contagious laughter always inspire me; Sarah Jones, who along with daughter Jenna vetted this content for me; and, of course, my sweet friend Julia Ryan, who has made every True Girl project "positively" beautiful with her design and illustration. Thank you, friends.

Being A True Girl

❝ *Hey, I wanna tell you something, but you **hafta promise** not to tell anyone."*
You lean in. You can hardly wait to hear what she's going to tell you.

Secrets. The juicy ones, the shocking ones, the embarrassing ones. There's something extra thrilling about hearing a friend's confession. Or getting the courage to tell your own.

❝ *My mom is gonna have **another baby**! But we aren't telling **anyone** until Grandma's birthday because she's gonna be so excited and **we want to surprise her!**"*

66 *I had head lice.* That's why I missed the school concert. It's so embarrassing!"

66 I got Jaycee the **best** birthday gift ever! *If you can keep a secret,* I'll tell you what it is!"

This book isn't about those kinds of secrets, but another kind. If you look in a dictionary, one of the definitions of the word *secret* is this:

When we use the word **secret** this way, we're saying that we have been taught how to do something or make something, or that we are an expert on a certain topic. Maybe you know

secret [see-krit] • *a method, formula, plan, etc., known only to the initiated or the few.*[1]

the secret to making a loom bracelet *without* a loom or a hook. Or perhaps your mom knows the secret to making your family's famous spaghetti sauce. Or you know the secret to multiplying by nine using your fingers. (That comes in handy for me, since I'm not the best at math!)

In this book, I'm going to introduce you to the seven secrets of true beauty and modesty. And I'm not going to tell them to you so you won't tell anyone else, but so you can keep them alive for the whole girl world.

Why Would You Want to Learn My Secrets?

Because a lot of girls are doing insanely bad things to try to feel more beautiful, and I don't want *you* to do those things!

Some girls spend every penny they can get on the latest beauty products.[2] (Don't do THAT!)

Some girls go on diets without telling their moms . . . when they're actually already *underweight!*[3] YIKES! (Don't do THAT!)

Some teenage girls get shots in their lips, making them as big as a watermelon! (Don't do THAT!)

Some girls wear shirts or pants that are too tight, skirts that are too short, and tops that are too low! (Don't do THAT!)

Here's the thing: **it's not working.**
It's been proven over and over again that those things don't make a girl feel better about herself. In fact, I've heard that most women or girls who spend time looking at fashion websites or magazines actually end up feeling more depressed about their own bodies. Who wouldn't? Little of what you see in those magazines is real. The girls are all "lighted," "touched-up," and "computer-generated" to "perfection" . . . a standard that's **IMPOSSIBLE** for you or me . . . or even the model in the picture!

Using the world's standards and ways of beauty to make you feel better about yourself is like trying to quench your thirst with an empty bottle. You're only going to stay thirsty while you become crazy out of your mind wondering why this water bottle is such a bummer!

More importantly, there are things God doesn't want us to do. He wants us to turn away from some choices. In other words, "Don't do that!"

> *"God wants us to turn from godless living and sinful pleasures and to live good, God-fearing lives day after day."* (Titus 2:12 TLB)

OK so a little lip gloss doesn't sound like a "sinful pleasure," and a super cute dress is not "godless living." And I want to be really clear: they aren't sinful pleasures! In fact, when my publisher first asked me to write about modesty and true beauty, I said, "No way!" I am a girl who really likes to "shop 'til you drop!" I like fashion, and I was a little afraid of what I might discover in the Bible if I started writing about modesty! Did God want to take away my sense of style?

If you are afraid of this book like I once was, relax! I found out that God didn't want to take away my desire to express my beauty. In fact, the one true God continually expresses Himself through beauty. (A sunset over an ocean or the colors of a peacock's tail are two things that come to my mind as beautiful expressions of God's creation.) It's no wonder that we want to do the same thing!

So, grab the cute dress. Sew some funky patches onto your worn-out jeans. Have a facial night with your BFF! These things aren't bad or sinful in and of themselves, but **BE CAREFUL** about *why* you like them. This is where many a girl has gone nearly insane with insecurity about how she looks and obsessions over brand names! If the reason you need them is to make you feel beautiful, then you've got a big problem, girl-friend! An interest in fashion and beauty can go wrong and become sinful, as I'll show you later in the book. *The bottom line is that fashion is not where true beauty comes from.* But I know where it does come from. And I know the seven secrets that will help you find it so that you will feel confident and aaamazing!

And I'm going to share them with you (and your mom if you're using the *True Girl Mom-Daughter Devos with Coloring Experience*).

AS YOU READ THIS BOOK, I WILL HELP YOU:

 improve YOUR understanding of true beauty & modesty.

 increase YOUR awareness of true beauty WITHIN YOU and YOUR contentment with the way that God chose to make you.

 renew YOUR love relationship with Jesus.

You will **KNOW** that you're beautiful just as you are, and you'll know **WHY**.

You will **LEARN** how to recognize lies about yourself and your beauty.

You will **GET CREATIVE** when you dress, fearless of the latest trends & careful in how you present yourself.

You will feel **POWERFUL** when you embrace modesty, because it allows the real you to shine!

♥ (Did I mention that you'll feel *aaamazing*?)

It's time to initiate you into the secrets of true beauty and modesty so you can be an official True Girl! Let's do it.

SECRETS

When You Shouldn't KEEP Them!!!

· ·

The secrets this book is about are the good kind. There are also neutral kinds of secrets: like keeping a surprise party secret or telling your friend that you've always dreamed of being a singer. Those are good secrets.

But there are also bad secrets. Here are three times when you definitely should not keep a secret.

1 When You're Hiding Something and Constantly Fearful Someone Will Find Out

If you worry all the time and even plan your life around a secret, it's time to spill the beans. If you won't accept your BFF's sleepover invites because you still sleep with a nightlight, just get it out there! Say something like, "Okay, but you should know I'm bringing my Sponge Bob Square Pants Nightlight. I never leave home without it." Your friend will laugh and you'll take your nightlight to her house and the secret will die, *but you* **WILL NOT!**

Or maybe the secret is something you did and you don't want anyone to know. If you're the one who spilled a juice box all over your mom's white carpet, it's time to 'fess up! There may be consequences but it'll be over eventually, and the pain of hiding something will be too.

2 When Your Friend Tells You a Secret You Don't Know How to Help With

Let's say it's 2:00 in the morning, and everyone at your sleepover party has long passed out. Only your bestie is hanging in with you as you swallow Sour Patch Kids in an effort to stay awake to finish one last movie. Suddenly she whispers, "I want to tell you a secret, but you have to promise not to tell anyone."

She tells you this is the first time in a week she hasn't spent the night all alone because her parents have been leaving her alone at night! Or maybe that she's been using social media and has discovered some really bad stuff. Or that her parents are getting a divorce and she wants your advice on how to stop it.

Should you **keep** her secret?

Sometimes secrets are too big and heavy for you to carry alone. When that happens, you have a responsibility to tell your mom or dad or another safe adult you trust a lot. And if your friend is in danger, you need to do it really fast! They'll be able to help you carry the big secret and help your friend.

3 When Someone Does Something to You and Makes You Promise Not to Tell

"This will be our little secret." Or "no one needs to ever know about this."
If anyone, especially an older person, tells you something like that before they do something with you or to you—or before they show you something that makes you uncomfortable—that is a green light to run as fast as you can to the nearest safe adult. It's a very brave and courageous thing to tell a secret like this. I'm so proud when I hear one of my True Girls has done this. Stopping someone like that doesn't just keep you safe, but it can keep other girls—and boys—safe too! We've got to stick together.

SECRETS will always be around.
There's no **end** to them,
but **you** can be **wise** about
knowing **which** ones to **keep**
and which ones **not** to!

1

The Master Artist

[You are a masterpiece created by God.]

Worst Day Ever!!!!!!! Today at school everyone was whispering and staring at me. So I went to the bathroom and right there on the tip of my nose was my first zit. I couldn't get a little cute one, like Laney Douglas' last week. (Hers looked like a beauty mark!) NOOOOOO! Mine is red like Elmo and swollen like a bloated whale. Getting ready for school in the morning used to take five minutes and now it seems like five hours couldn't fix my face! I'm a disaster! It's not like I want to be a lip-gloss addicted beauty queen or anything, but do I have to look like THIS? —Yuzi

...right on the tip of my nose!

ave you ever thought any bad things about yourself when you look in the mirror? Well, have you? Let's be honest. You have. And I have too. We're girls, and the whole girl world has experienced the phenomenon known as a bad hair day. And don't even get me started on zits. You know what I think? That God doesn't want us to think those thoughts, and that He really is sad for us when we write them down or worry about them all day long.

The Bible tells us that when God looks down upon you, he is *"enthralled* by your beauty"! (Psalm 45:11 NIV). The word enthralled means He is captivated, delighted, fascinated, charmed, enchanted BY YOU.

He can't take His eyes off of you. True fact. Psalm 17:8 says you are the "apple of [His] eye." That means that if you were to look into God's eye and see the reflection of what He was looking at, it would be YOU!

Wow! Think of that. The God of the universe, looking down at your uniquely chiseled features, coloring, and size, keeps His eyes on you because you are one of His treasured creations . . . He thinks you're beautiful.

So why can't you believe it? Well, somewhere along the way, someone decided to redefine beauty. Right now the standard of beauty is to be as tall as a basketball player and as thin as a pencil. (And don't forget those lips the size of a watermelon.) It's an impossible standard, and as we'll soon discover, the standard of beauty today is a big fat lie!

Here's the deal: no one is both as tall as a basketball player and as thin as a pencil. A tall basketball player's beauty is in her strength. A thin girl's beauty is in her delicate frame, but she isn't necessarily going to be tall! And I'm not sure why people want unnaturally fat lips. (When God makes lips nice and full, they are beautiful! But when we try to fake it, they just look swollen.) If I see you with swollen lips, I'll assume you ate something you were super allergic to. Unless of course God created you with full lips, because then they'll fit your face nicely and you'll be adored for them!

Each of us is different. Every girl has her own special appearance, and there is no mistake in how you turned out. How do I know this? Because I know the first secret—and you're about to know it too!

🌼 Secret #1: You are a masterpiece created by God!

Genesis 1:1 reads,
"In the beginning, God created . . ."

Like an artist, He set out to make a beautiful world.

Let's go back to the garden of Eden, where God made the first girl, Eve. Oh wait! Back up. Let's enter the garden just *before* He creates Eve.

Check it out. In Genesis 1, God surveys His fine creation and finds everything just right. He uses the word *good*. The aardvark is good. The aloe plant is good. The alpaca is good. The amoeba is good. The artichoke is good. (And I'm just on the A's, but you get the idea.) *Everything* is good . . . with one exception. He says, "It is *not* good for man to be alone."

Hold it one minute there. Did you catch that? **Alone?** The God of the universe was walking and talking with Adam. How could Adam have been *alone*? God could've easily just been Adam's BFF. He didn't choose to be. Instead, He crafted a masterpiece . . . woman! You are one of those masterpieces. Oh, what a

GOD is a master artist and He created you! THAT MAKES **YOU** A MASTERPIECE!

masterpiece you are! Like the famous Mona Lisa at the Louvre Museum in Paris or a fine Picasso painting on display in Barcelona, Spain, you're a masterpiece worthy of every glance that comes your way!

And there's a lot of glancing going on. Check this out: advertising researchers have actually attached little sensors to readers' eyeballs to follow the visual path and figure out what makes someone spend time reading an ad, increasing an advertiser's chance of sales. Crazy, huh? They've discovered lots of little tricks that will increase the viewing time by 1% . . . 2% . . . maybe 3%. But if you really want to stop the reader, use a woman. I've heard different numbers, but it seems a photo of a woman will increase the length of time someone spends with an ad by up to 30%. That's way more than anything else. It didn't matter much whether it was a woman or a man doing the looking. Both were drawn to the beauty of the female image.

CRAZY, HUH?

Advertisers just don't get the same response when they use the image of a man, no matter how fantastic looking he might be. It's the masterpiece called "woman" that calls our eyes to praise. The masterpiece is applauded by our glances.

You were created as a masterpiece, and **you** are one of God's expressions of beauty. Short, tall; thin, thick; freckles; big eyes, small ones . . . it doesn't matter. The beauty of being an artist is making things that are **DIFFERENT!**

Take a look at these three paintings, and guess which one is by the world-famous painter **VINCENT** VAN **GOGH**.

The Potato Eaters

Starry Night

Sunflowers

Guess what? They're all by Vincent van Gogh! *The Potato Eaters* is considered van Gogh's first great work of art. (What's not great about something named *The Potato Eaters*!?) *Starry Night* may be his most famous. (Does it look familiar to you?) *Sunflowers* is from his famous still life collection. But each of these is unique in style and use of color. (*The Potato Eaters* is very realistic and dark. *Starry Night* is very unrealistic and used bright colors. *Sunflowers* is kind of in between, realistic but bright.)

Each of them is a masterpiece because they were painted by a master painter.

YOU are a masterpiece created by GOD.

Why are you a masterpiece?
Simply because you were created by
THE Master Artist!

Is it hard for you to believe you are a masterpiece? Do you think you are too tall? Too short? Too heavy? Too thin? Is your hair too curly? Too straight? Too dark? Too light? Yeah, I know how it feels to be different from everyone around you. And how desperate you can become to do something about it!

When I was in sixth grade, every-one in the entire wide world—yep, I'm being dramatic—was getting their hair cut into "feathers." A stylist would cut the hair around your face at an angle so you could brush it back into wispy "feathers" to frame your face. It was *the* style of the day. I had long, straight, blonde hair at the time, and it felt so boring compared to everyone else's. I begged my mom to take me to get it cut. When we did, it didn't go as planned! My hair just didn't want to "feather." Instead it coiled into heavy, greasy-looking curls at the side. I cried myself to sleep a night or two. I felt so ugly.

Determined to fix it, I told my mom that what I now needed was a "perm." Also the rage of the day! My mom said we couldn't afford a salon perm, so I begged and begged and begged until she relented to give me a "home perm." She tightly coiled all my hair into rollers until my eyes teared up and I felt I might not make it through. Then she poured what can only be described as a toxic liquid on my head. I'm pretty sure you could smell me on the other side of the earth. I smelled bad and I looked even worse, but this was going to be what made me beautiful! I could just feel it!

But *feelings are not facts*. Only the Bible can give us the real facts on true beauty. So how about we start there.

Bible **True Beauty** Fact #1

The Bible says one thing that makes a woman beautiful is being different or unique (Song of Solomon 6:9). No matter **WHAT** is different about you, you are a masterpiece created by God. It's not only okay to be taller, shorter, thicker, thinner, curlier, straighter, darker, or lighter, but it is also **BEAUOOO**-tiful! Different is good! (An art gallery full of masterpieces would get so boring so fast if every single one of them were the same, right?)

Bible **True Beauty** Fact #2

The Bible also tells us that a girl in love with Jesus **knows** she's a masterpiece!
"Wait!" you might be saying. "That sounds kind of prideful."
So let me put it to you the way the Bible does.
The Bible says a girl who knows Jesus knows **very well** that she is a masterpiece.
That's a lot of knowing. Let me show you where that shows up in the pages of the Bible:

. . . .

Secret #1 Power Verse

"I praise you, for I am fearfully and wonderfully made.
Wonderful are your works; my soul knows it very well.
My frame was not hidden from you, when I was being
made in secret, intricately woven . . ."

(Psalm 139:14–15)

. . . .

This verse says that God, the Master Artist, wove you together when you were still in the womb. Have you ever worked on a weaving loom? Or knitted or crocheted? If you have, you know that you don't just throw a blob of yarn together and say, "Well, would you look at that? Somehow I made a hat!" It takes careful attention to detail to weave something together. It can't happen on accident. It takes counting. Math!

What does that mean for you? Every single thing about you was made *carefully.*
God calculated the length of your legs. The width of your nose. The curl in your
hair. He's even counted the numbers of hairs on your head (Luke 12:7). He decided
what color your eyes should be. And what shade of that color. He chose your skin
color and the curves in your bones. You are His piece of art.

God does not make junk. He makes masterpieces. And He wants you to know
"**very well**" that you're a masterpiece.

Why are you a masterpiece? That's simple: to make the Master Artist known.
Our primary purpose on this earth is to glorify—or to make known—God. All
this creative genius expressed in you is not to make you famous, but to make God

famous! (Is this starting to
make any sense?)

Let's go back to Vincent
van Gogh's work for a
minute. He had a unique way
of signing his work. He only
signed "Vincent." Sometimes
it was really big like on this
painting at the Van Gogh
Museum in Amsterdam.

Seascape-at-Saintes-Maries
by Vincent van Gogh

Van Gogh's Chair by Vincent Van Gogh

Sometimes it was put in an unusual place like on this painting of his chair. See if you can find his name.

See it back there on the drawer? Now look back at Sunflowers by van Gogh and find the unique spot he placed his name on that one! Find it?

All of these paintings tell us "Vincent was here!"

You tell the world "God was here! God is here!"

It is your mission, should you choose to accept it, to let the whole world know that you are a masterpiece created by God so that the whole world will know God is the Master Artist!

I really wish I had known this powerful secret before I begged my mom for a perm. Oh yeah, that story didn't turn out so well. My mom had, in fact, rolled the rollers too tightly. So tightly that one of the rollers actually worked with those harsh chemicals to literally shave a spot right on top of my head. At first I could hide it, but as the hair grew, there was a sprout of perfectly straight hair standing proudly on the top of my head. I looked so ridiculous, thanks to my obsession with a hairstyle! If only I had accepted the mission to let the whole world know that God created me very well . . . long, straight hair and all!

Now, let me remind you of something I said earlier. Curling your hair when it's straight or straightening your hair when it is curly is not

HAIR FUN!

bad in and of itself. Have fun! Braid it. Cut it. Curl it. Even color it if your mom thinks that's okay. But make sure that you don't lose sight of the fact that the way God created you is good, and your beauty enables the world to see our Master Artist. It's something He hopes we'll participate in with as much energy (or more) as we use to be creative with our expression of beauty when it comes to our hair!

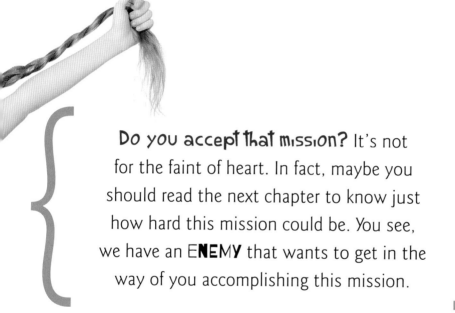

{ **Do you accept that mission?** It's not for the faint of heart. In fact, maybe you should read the next chapter to know just how hard this mission could be. You see, we have an **ENEMY** that wants to get in the way of you accomplishing this mission. }

2

The Counterfeiter

[True beauty doesn't come from what's on the outside.]

It was the worst, most-embarrassing moment in the history of all most-embarrassing moments! Laney

...white cotton ball thingies!

Douglas was totally showing off in gym class today. (Probably because Zachary Donaldson, a HIGH SCHOOL FOOTBALL PLAYER, was in the gym working out when we were there!) We were playing volleyball and she jumped up to reach the ball but so did my amazing friend Toni Diaz. When it was over, they were a mangled mess of arms and legs AND ONE LITTLE GLARING CLUMP OF WHITE COTTON BALL THINGIES . . . snagged on Laney's t-shirt!

Toni grabbed it and handed it to her. I've never seen Laney run so fast. I think she ran to the locker room and Mrs. Penland didn't even stop her. People were saying that cotton ball thingy was from her bra! Is it possible that Laney Douglas actually stuffs her bra to look bigger??? :o Sigh! Maybe I'm not that far behind everyone else. (I still want my mom to take me BRA SHOPPING!!!)

—Kate

Here's something I really should tell you: **We are women. We have breasts.** And just like the other parts of us, these will be unique and different from the next person. And yours will grow at a different rate than every other girl you'll ever meet. And they'll end up different, too. This *could* cause no small amount of frustration! You see, most of the bad things we think about ourselves happen when we *compare ourselves to other girls*. (Don't do *that!*)

Thinking bad things about ourselves leads to *doing* insane and silly things.

For example, a very long time ago in Italy, *where God created people to have dark, olive-colored skin*, women wanted to have lighter skin like other women they saw from other countries. They began to use a white powder called arsenic to lighten themselves. SIX HUNDRED WOMEN DIED because arsenic is a poison. Hello! (That's insane!)

That may sound crazy to you and me, but is it really that much different from buying overly padded bras or stuffing your bra with cotton or tissues to look bigger than you are? **(That's silly!)**

tissues for your nose!

If we are masterpieces created by God, we will understand that we do not need to change ourselves with makeup and padded bras. (Okay, it's important to know that sometimes a little padding in your bra is helpful to be modest or to fit properly in an outfit, *but if you're doing it simply to look bigger, something is wrong*.) We don't need clothes, make up, jewelry, fancy hairstyles, and padded bras to make us feel good about ourselves. I said it once, and I'll say it again: there is nothing really wrong with using those things appropriately to express our personal sense of style and to enhance our beauty, but sometimes we become dependent on them *for the purpose of feeling better about ourselves*. We get confused. We think those things are actually what make us beautiful.

To be honest, I think all of us have had moments when we feel like we'll be beautiful if we just have a certain pair of jeans or a specific haircut. If you've had that feeling, you're not alone. **That's why we need secret number TWO.**

Secret #2: True beauty does not come from what's on the outside.

E ven though the Bible was written way before blue jeans were the universal statement of style and manicure parties were the rage, God knew they were coming. He knew that as fun as they are, they might tempt us to believe that we *had* to have them to be beautiful. More than two thousand years ago, He had the apostle Peter write this so we would not do silly and insane things.

. . . .

Secret #2 Power Verse

"Your beauty should not come from outward adornment,
such as elaborate hairstyles and the wearing of gold
jewelry or fine clothes." (I Peter 3:3 NIV)

. . . .

OK Let's think: is this verse saying we should all run around naked? No. That'd be completely awkward! Of course God wants us to wear clothing. So if we know that this isn't saying "no clothes," it is also clear that it's *not* saying "no cute hair" and "no jewelry."

The point of this verse is not to make us dress like pioneer women with bonnets and long, poofy dresses! Beauty and fashion aren't bad. If you ask me, God liked expressing Himself with beautiful things. In the book of Revelation, God is described. Things we consider to be beautiful surround Him in John's vision of heaven. Revelation 4:3 says that God sat on His throne, and He was so amazingly beautiful that the writer said He "had the appearance of jasper . . . and around the throne was a rainbow that had the appearance of an emerald." Moses actually saw God's beauty, in part. God's glory was so powerful that Moses had to settle for seeing the back of God. Afterward, Moses's face literally glowed from how powerful God's presence was.

BEA**UTY** is one of God's greatest expressions.

I think it's only fitting that we, created in His image, love expressing our beauty too. So, express it! Use press-on nails. Paint your toes. Find the world's most adorable skirt. Rock a pair of jeans and a graphic T-shirt. Learn to braid. Pop on some lip gloss. Start a bracelet collection. It's okay.

So what IS the point of that power verse? It's to remind us that as fun as fashion and beauty products are, **they are not what make you beautiful!**

[Your beauty does not come from what's on the outside.]

That hardly makes sense to us because we live in a world where we are constantly seeing advertising messages that seem to tell us we cannot be

A PIERCING QUESTION

"Is it okay for me to [fill in the blank]?"

Throughout this book I make a lot of fun references to things like "using press-on nails," "coloring your hair," or "sewing patches onto your jeans." Those are things you should run through your family preference filter. (And by that I mean your mom or dad.) The Bible tells us to honor and obey our parents, so you might have to wait for some things. I wasn't allowed to get my ears pierced until I was 18! But it sure felt good to submit to my dad's preference in that area of my life, and it was super fun the day I finally got to have them pierced!

beautiful unless our hair is cut a certain way or we own a certain brand of jeans or we have the latest trend in jewelry. The message is that what is on the outside is what actually determines our beauty. It's a lie!

Where do those beauty lies come from?

I'm glad you asked!

Do you believe in good and evil? I do. Most of the world does. I mean, show me the civilization that gives out trophies for being a lily-livered coward! That would not make sense to anyone. But almost every civilization recognizes and rewards great lion-hearted courage.[4] That's because humans believe in right and wrong. Good and evil.

We grew up hearing stories that were filled with good guys and bad guys. *Star Wars* and *Cinderella* and *The Lion, the Witch, and the Wardrobe* might not look like they have anything in common.

One is full of star ships and space creatures. One is full of castles and ball gowns. One has talking animals. But they do have something in common: a battle between good and evil. Although these stories are not real, I believe good and evil are very real. Why do I believe that? Because the Bible tells me they are.

Through the Bible, we learn who leads the forces of good and evil.

The Lord God Almighty, our Master Artist, is good (Psalm 119:68).

Satan is a powerful angel who rebelled against God because he wanted to be more powerful than God. He is in a constant battle against God. He is evil (Isaiah 14:12–15).

What did Satan want? To be like God. He is a counterfeiter. That is to say, he seeks to be a fake imitation of the Master Artist.

counterfeit

[koun-ter-fit] • an imitation intended to be passed off... deceptively as genuine.[5]

Here's a strange BUT true story

There's actually a guy who is a pretty good artist named Mark Landis. He's soooooo good, hardly anybody can tell his paintings from the works of famous master artists. (He makes them by painting over copies and pictures of the real things!) Would you believe that he's tricked sixty museums in twenty states when he donated art to them and told them it was actually by a famous artist? In reality, it was painted in his own house by his own hand! He is a counterfeiter. Even though the museum staff carefully examined the paintings, they were fooled. Mark Landis was *that* good when it came to being a counterfeiter! He spent a lot of his life trying to pretend his work was in the name of other master artists.

If God is the Master Artist, Satan is the master counterfeiter. But while Mark Landis isn't an evil man and meant no real harm with the art he created, Satan is very evil and can create a lot of damage in our lives. The Bible says that if we could see him, he would not look evil at all. "Satan disguises himself as an angel of light" (2 Corinthians 11:14).

Satan is not only good at making fakes, but he is good at *faking you out!* He tries to convince you that you are *not* a master-piece when you really, truly are.

There's one thing you must know about the counterfeiter above all else: he cannot be trusted! The Bible says, "There is no truth in him. When he lies, he speaks out of his own character, for he is a liar and the father of lies" (John 8:44). One of his favorite things to lie to you about is your value! He wants to convince you that you are NOT a masterpiece created by the Master Artist. If he can do that, the world won't see you and remember God. Remember, that's the true purpose of your beauty . . . to remind people, "God was here! God is here!"

Expect to be lied to when it comes to beauty in general. Case in point: almost ANY photo you see on the Internet, billboards, posters, advertisements . . . is one big fat LIE! The tricks of the trade really have to be SEEN to be believed . . . so let me introduce you to the leading photo-altering program, Photoshop. Using it, we can make almost anything look real. Check this out:

Did you know you could ride roosters?

You didn't? Well, of course you can't! That's a picture of me riding a horse combined with a picture of my crazy rooster, Franklin. My designer friend, Julia, put them together, and suddenly I'm riding a rooster!

Cock-a-doodle-WHO?

ALENA is not only the young star in *War Room*, but also (along with her amazing mom Wynter) a new author of some fabulous fiction books under the series name *Lena in the Spotlight*. Check them out!

The lies we see about beauty are very subtle, but no less real. And I'll take this photo of my beautiful and perfect-just-as-she-is friend, Alena Pitts, who was the young star of the *War Room* movie with her auntie Priscilla Shirer.

Let's make her look different using Photoshop. We've thickened her hair, widened her eyes, and changed her cheekbones. This isn't real! (And frankly, I like the REAL Alena better than the fake one!)

The Real ALENA

ALENA Photoshopped

YIKES! This is crazy, right? Sadly, a lot of the photos you see in ads and even on Instagram are equally fake!

More than a few famous advertisers have gotten into a lot of trouble when its designers went too far with Photoshop. Often these models end up looking so skinny they don't even look real. They take way too much away for us to be fooled.

This is **JUST** ridiculous! Don't you agree??? Girls, you don't have to change yourself to be beautiful!!! You are perfectly crafted just the way you are.

So, if beauty doesn't come from our hairstyles, jewelry, and fashion, where does it come from? I'm so glad you asked! It's one of the most important things a girl can know, and it's our **THIRD** secret.

Franklin, the rooster, and me riding Truett before I transformed into the . . .
Notorious Chicken Rider of the East!

3

The Confusion

[True beauty is not about how you look. It's about how you see.]

What ON EARTH happened to me??? As far as I can tell the earth opened up and swallowed my fashion-obsessed brain. The next thing I knew my

...no idea what happened!

heart grew two sizes, and I was throwing the pageant. You know the pageant I was BORN TO WIN . . . the one I've been waiting for since before I could talk. I have no idea what happened to me back-stage. But I just saw things differently, like some-one put super mega-powered vision glasses on me and I could see right into Riley Peterson's inner being. Her dress didn't meet the pageant rules! How could she have missed it? I knew one thing: she needed my one-of-a-kind Cinderella-worthy dress way more than I did. So, before I knew it I was wearing her dress—the one that got me disqualified. And she was wearing my show stopper! The Miss Teeny Pop Crown will never be mine. (And don't tell anyone, but I feel pretty good about that!) —Danika

Where DOES real beauty come from if you can't buy it at the mall? We've already learned that it *doesn't* come from the outside, right? So, we've got to go much farther than the mall and deeper than your closet to find something that will make you truly beautiful. For one thing, what people think is beautiful on the outside is always changing.

Fashion trends change from culture to culture and season to season. Sometimes the things one culture finds appealing make another laugh. In Madagascar, a woman's exposed arms were once considered very sexy, so you were a *wild* woman if you wore short sleeves.

In the Bible we read that a nose ring was presented to Rebekah as a sort of engagement ring when she agreed to marry Isaac. It said way more than "marry me." It also said, "I'm rich." A nose ring was reserved for the upper class and was a sign

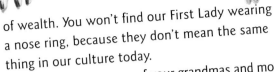

of wealth. You won't find our First Lady wearing a nose ring, because they don't mean the same thing in our culture today.

More recently, some of your grandmas and moms were wearing what we know as "ugly sweaters." (Only they didn't think they were so ugly!)

All I'm saying is that what is in style today might be something you laugh at in just a few years. Girls, we've got to stop getting so obsessed with what we look like on the outside. The world WILL keep spinning if your jeans don't have the most popular name brand on them! You can't measure beauty simply by what is or is not on the body. True beauty comes from deep inside of you.

You remember that power verse from the last chapter? It said: "Your beauty should not come from outward adornment, such as elaborate hairstyles and the wearing of gold jewelry and fine clothes." Get ready for the verse that comes right after it, because it's your next power verse. (You can't fully understand one without the other!)

. . . .

Secret #3 Power Verse

*"Be beautiful inside, in your hearts, with the
lasting charm of a gentle and quiet spirit that is
so precious to God."* (1 Peter 3:4 TLB)

. . . .

When you see these verses together, it's even more apparent that God isn't dissing fashion so much as He is calling you and me to a deeper, truer beauty than we can get at the mall.

The fashion **INSIDE OF US** is what makes us **GORGEOUS** in the eyes of God! Oh, yes, you can wear "clothes" on the inside like kindness . . . helpfulness . . . encouragement . . . love . . . forgiveness . . . and so much more! **THESE** are the things **GOD** thinks are fashionable. And He likes it when we accessorize with some laughter . . . and hugs . . . and high fives for each other!

Unlike fashion and external beauty, our power verse says that inner beauty is "lasting." Some versions of the Bible say it is "unfading." This *could partly* be referring to the fact that we're all gonna get older some day and this changes the way we look, but I think it has very little to do with age. This is something worth exploring, so let's pretend you know two identical twins. Physically, they look like the same person. Not a thing about them is different, down to the itty, bitty beauty mark on their right cheek and the funky zig-zag part their hair naturally falls into. Both of them are dressed well and physically attractive, but there *are* some differences . . . *beneath* their skin.

Twin #1: Fading Beauty

Twin number one is a mean girl. She's this way mostly because she's insecure and jealous and doesn't really like herself nearly as much as she pretends. When she looks in the mirror each day, she obsesses over how she looks, and she HAS to have designer jeans or she'd just die of embarrassment. On a daily basis, she's worried about who likes her, but she wouldn't notice a lonely classmate if she had super vision x-ray glasses. She's much too busy looking out for herself to see the needs of others. The more time you spend around her, the more something happens to the way she appears to you. **Her beauty fades.**

> { External beauty is hard to see over **INTERNAL UGLY!** }

Have you ever met someone like this whose stunning looks *fade* as her personality comes through? Then you've seen the girl who lacks true beauty. External beauty is hard to see over internal ugly!

Twin #2: Unfading Beauty

Twin number two is sweet, kind, and helpful. She's confident in who she is, so she doesn't spend much time in front of the mirror worrying about how she looks, and she likes the challenge of finding a bargain when it comes to fashion because she knows it helps her mom and dad afford other things. A lot of people like her because she's always making others feel important. She does this by seeing their needs and helping them. The more you spend time around her, the more beautiful she becomes.

Have you ever met a girl who becomes more and more attractive as you get to know her? If you know a person like this, you've seen true beauty. External beauty shines brighter when inner beauty is growing!

{ External beauty shines brighter when **INNER BEAUTY** is growing! }

These girls look 100% the same to our physical eyes, but the one wearing beautiful inner garments has a beauty that lasts and is unfading. And the one who is wearing ugly inner garments has a beauty that fades away. What's the difference? It's not in the way they look. (They're identical twins!) It's in the way that they SEE!

Secret #3: True beauty is not about how you look. It's about how you see.

True beauty has very little to do with how we *look*—our skin, our hair, our legs, our eyes, our figure, and more. It's got everything to do with how we *see* the needs of others. God's Word reads, "Let each of you look not only to his own interests, but also to the interests of others" (Philippians 2:4).

God wants you to have His eyes to see the needs of others before your

own needs! This is true beauty. He wants you to be less worried about how you look and more concerned with how you see. The only way you'll grow that skill is to spend more time working on your inner beauty than your outer beauty.

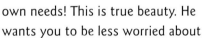

HAVE **HIS** EYES TO **SEE!**

My daughter Autumn is a true beauty. Not only did God carefully craft her lovely face—her perky nose and full lips are so sweet—and tiny little body, but He planted beautiful things in her heart. When she was thirteen, one of our favorite families broke up. No other way to say it. Mom left and dad was alone with several children. Autumn **SAW** this suddenly single dad's need.

USE THE EYES OF YOUR HEART!

Often she would ask if we were making him food and if we could help them with their home. She has great vision, and that's where true beauty comes from: your eyes! Not really your physical eyes so much as what the Bible calls the "eyes of your heart" (Ephesians 1:18).

In the same way—if God has marriage in your future, I want a guy to be attracted to your beauty by what he "sees" in your heart and mind. If he is attracted to your internal beauty, he'll also find the physical expression God has crafted in you to be beautiful, too! (Even when you get old and it's beginning to fade away . . . but that's all a long time away.)

I'm going to help you with your vision in just a few short chapters, but for now I want to introduce you to some real live girls who have excellent vision. (Read: true beauty!) Turn the page to the next chapter for a fashion show of the **"INNER"** kind.

4

Protecting the Masterpiece

[God wants nothing we wear to distract people from seeing our true beauty.]

I was totally sprawled on the ground with no hope of saving a scrap of I-meant-to-do-that-ness. I wished I could snap my fingers and disappear!

...wish I could disappear!

For a millisecond I thought maybe no one would notice the girl lying face-down dressed in a tight, itchy, horrible corncob costume. Yep! My mom dressed me like a COB OF CORN for the annual Popcorn Festival. She thought I would make a good greeter and that it was my duty to God and country to volunteer. She says we're all supposed to do good deeds. But what I did was make a mess because that silly costume was impossible to walk in. My only hope is that the costume was too distracting for people to notice WHO was actually in there! —Yuzi

I'd like to show you some masterpieces and tell you just one way that their true beauty shines.

REBECCA has been given what God calls in the book of Exodus "a spirit of skill" with fabrics. She makes beautiful clothes, bags, and other fabric items and shares them generously with other people. Her true beauty shines through her **GIVING!**

REBECCA BARKER

SHARIN ROCCO

ZAANI ANDERSON

SHARIN has a true "gentle and quiet" spirit, which we learned about in our power verses. I've watched her interact with her group of True Girls in the Dominican Republic and have been blessed by her quiet spirit. Her true beauty shines through her **LISTENING!**

ZAANI is the middle Anderson sister. Sometimes middle sisters get lost in the shuffle, but I watch Zaani confidently be the girl God made her to be while she lets her big sister, Sorochi, shine and helps her little sister, Ru, grow. Her true beauty shines through her **KINDNESS!**

JENNA JONES

JENNA loves the Lord, and her parents have been teaching her how to manage her weekly allowance to demonstrate it. When they asked her where she wanted to donate some, she prayed and felt led to give it to my True Girl Nation fund, which helps girls in need. Just a week later, a hurricane hit Haiti, and I was able to send Jenna's gift and the gifts of many others to help some girls whose home was damaged. Her true beauty shines through her **FAITH!**

These girls wear beautiful things *inside*. And that is precisely why they are careful with what they wear on the outside. Let me help you understand by using God's Word. Your next power verse sounds a lot like the verses we have been studying written by Peter. But the verses below are written by the apostle Paul and pack a punch of sheer power at the end.

Secret #4 Power Verse

*"I want women to be modest in their appearance.
They should wear decent and appropriate clothing and
not draw attention to themselves by the way they
fix their hair or by wearing gold or pearls or expensive
clothes. For women who claim to be devoted to
God should make themselves attractive by the good
things they do."* (1 Timothy 2:9–10 NLT)

There it is again: the truth that what makes us attractive is inner beauty, which gives us vision to SEE the needs of others and do good things to help them. The purpose of this verse once again is to push us into goodness, not to make a lot of rules about our clothes.

IS IT OKAY?

But it *does* mention clothes. And it says they should be *appropriate*. Appropriate means being able to say, "It's okay!" So let's see if some of these things are appropriate.

Let's start simple: is it okay to wear a party dress to a campfire? Come on, now. People would think you were fairly odd! There's nothing really wrong with it, but if your mom spent a lot of money on that dress and you came home covered in gray ash, she may be frustrated with you. It's just not appropriate to wear a party dress to a campfire. It is appropriate to wear some jeans and a sweatshirt!

modesty

[mod-uh-stee] • *presenting your external beauty so carefully that it does not distract people from seeing the good things you do, but empowers your true beauty to shine*

Now, let's go in another direction with this question.

Is it okay to wear your swimming suit to church? Now, this is starting to feel a little uncomfortable for people around you because you just don't have enough fabric covering you, right? (Of course, this example is so extreme, it sounds more silly than anything.)

Now, let's get to the heart of the Bible verse. Is it okay to wear an itty-bitty skirt that's so unbelievably short that it shows your panties when you bend over to pick something up? Uhm! No! Now, things are getting way too revealing. It's inappropriate and draws attention to a girl in a way that is not okay.

But each and every day the world is making it normal for you and me to be inappropriate. That is: to wear things that are **NOT OKAY**! Of course, I haven't seen anyone wearing a Speedo to worship, but I've seen plenty of super-short skirts on girls. You know what I mean?

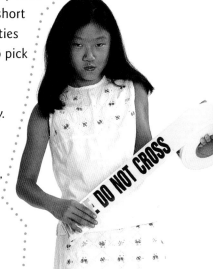

God gives us specific instruction not to wear something that is immodest or inappropriate. Why? Not because He likes making up lots of rules about clothes, but because He wants nothing about the way we dress to distract from the good work that we do for Him. That's why we have to be careful and appropriate in the way that we dress. It's time to talk about the power of modesty!

Modesty is a power that protects the ability of others to see God's good works in your heart and through your life.

It is not meant to hide your body, but to reveal the true beauty that grows within you.

Immodesty carelessly reveals too much of your body and distracts people from seeing what's inside of you! *It takes away the power of your inner beauty.* You see, the power of modesty is that it lets people see inside of you. But there's a lot of immodesty in our world. In fact, it's more normal to see a lot of girls who are immodest than it is to see a lot of girls doing good things for other people.

WARNING:

Some people make modesty all about a lot of rules for our bodies. "Your skirt should be two inches above your knee." My definition of modesty is a bit different because I think it has a whole lot more to do with our hearts and why we choose a skirt, not how long it is. You won't find this definition in a dictionary, but I believe it expresses God's definition of modesty accurately.

A Brief History of Modern Immodesty[6]

Fashion has always been cycling from modest to immodest. Here's a look at how the progression goes.

It All Began with a Dress

1913 • Rounded & V-Shaped Necklines After a season of strict modesty accompanied by ordinary dresses having high collars, clergymen all over the world jumped into their pulpits to condemn the new rounded and high v-necklines women were sporting. (Gasp!)

1918 • Pants

When World War I hit, so did a fashion item that had been trying to catch on since fourth-century Persia: women's pants. Since women needed to go into factories to do men's jobs, this time the fashion statement stuck. Loose pants and riding pants were the rage!

1920 • Flapper Dresses

For the first time, dresses were short . . . and women were showing ARMS & LEGS! "Flappers," what the girls who wore these dresses were called, were known to attend "necking parties" where they randomly kissed any guy they met. The dress, though modest by today's standards, was a symbol of their rebellion.

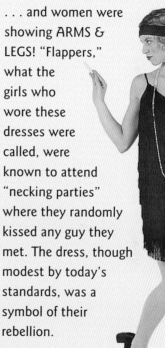

1960 • The Mini-Skirt

The mini-skirt was the first fashion item marketed directly at the teenager. Fashion designer Mary Quant saw that young women had to "dress like their mothers" and wanted to give them their own fashion sense. The skirt became a symbol of women's freedom and rebellion. (There's that word again.)

1970 • Bare Midriff

The West was finally introduced to the female belly button. Low-riders cantered in to pair up with shirts that showed off the curves of a woman's body, and became a fashion statement that comes and goes—almost as unstoppable as the mini-skirt.

2000 • Underwear as Outerwear

Underwear was no longer under anything. First glimpsing out over the low-cut collars of women, it slowly made its way to the surface. A camisole, bra, or thong "whale tail" was considered a fashion statement rather than an "oops!"

TODAY • Anything Goes

Taking a little from each fashion decade, today a girl can wear just about anything, and it's considered nothing more than an expression.

I need to confess to you that I've had some moments in my life when I gave up the power of modesty. I didn't protect my internal beauty by presenting my body carefully.

Once, I stood up in the front of my minivan, the door wide open, while I bent over the seat to reach my stuff. It was a loooong reach. As I turned to slam the door shut with my arms loaded, I noticed a guy sitting in his car right beside me with his jaw dropped so low that his mouth looked like the Grand Canyon. His face was red when I caught him staring.

THAT'S WHEN THE DRAFT HIT ME.

That's when the draft hit me. A cool spring breeze announced to me that the hem of my very short skirt was wrapped up around my waist and my panties were the featured view. You can guess who was blushing then!

Let me tell you that no one who saw my lacy underwear was going to notice that I was a good person who loved serving her community and doing good things for Jesus. My clothing distracted them from seeing the good things I did. I don't wear skirts that short anymore. Lesson learned! I have embraced the power of modesty. I want people to see the good things I do *because I want them to see Jesus in me.*

Modesty and the way it distracts us from seeing inside a person is actually quite scientific! Let me tell you about the Gestalt theory. (Warning: college-level thinking ahead! I believe you can handle it.) The Gestalt theory teaches an artist to control a viewer's time by forcing the person to mentally complete a visual image. Because the brain is intrigued by completing the incomplete, it will always pause to finish an unfinished picture. Check out this trio of circles. What else do you see?

You think you see a triangle, because that's the most common image that your brain wants to use to complete this.

Check out this next little graphic. Describe what you see.
People say they see a person, even though this is just a couple of curved lines and a dot. Why? We naturally seek to continue visual elements.

Now check out this photo of clouds in the sky. What do you see?
You probably have sat in the grass and looked up at clouds to find things and seen anything from a puppy, to a crown, to an alligator, or Jesus riding on a white horse. There's

a name for what's happening in your head. It's the Gestalt principle of continuity. (Now that's college student stuff, right there. We're smart!)

Now, let's apply that to the way we dress. What does someone see when a girl walks by wearing a long, tight skirt with a slit all the way up the sides? They see past the fabric, because the slit invites them to finish the picture. This is simple visual science.

When our imagination kicks in and we start being focused on a person's body, we have a hard time seeing their heart. That's how we get distracted from seeing a person's good deeds! (Does this start to make the POWER of modesty make some sense? You see, modesty is your choosing to control what a person sees: the outside of you or the inside!)

I think you're ready for secret #4.

> Secret #4: God wants nothing we wear to distract people from seeing our true beauty.

Now, don't go all "Little House on the Prairie" on me. Don't hide your body. That's not the purpose of God's instruction on modesty. After all, you are a masterpiece created by God, and masterpieces are made to be seen. You remind people of the Master Artist!

But your true beauty and value lies within you. And it is a treasure to be carefully protected. You must take care to present yourself as a valuable masterpiece.

curator

[kyoo-rey-ter] · the
person in charge
of a museum,
art collection, etc.[7]

As the protector of a masterpiece created by God, you are a curator! A curator is a person in charge of an art collection.

MASTERPIECES, you see, must be protected.

Take, for example, the *Mona Lisa*. She's considered the world's most famous painting and was completed by master artist Leonardo da Vinci in 1517. Today she is *curated* by The Louvre (pronounced "looove"), a famous museum in Paris, France. She's hidden behind a sealed bullet-proof glass enclosure that is almost two inches thick. The temperature inside is permanently set at 43 degrees Fahrenheit and 50% humidity. A tiny spotlight brings out the colors in the painting. During World War II, when art was often stolen by Nazi soldiers, the painting was hidden in five different locations. Though she once traveled to other countries for display, the curator says she will never again be lent out for exhibition, for her protection, due to the fact that she wasn't treated properly in other locations.

This is certainly more protection than she was given in 1911 when she was STOLEN. That's right, the captain of the guard came around to the location where she was kept on a few pegs, and she was simply gone. He didn't freak out or anything. (HELLO! FREAK OUT! IT'S THE WORLD'S MOST FAMOUS PAINTING!) He just assumed maybe someone had taken the painting out for cleaning or photographing for marketing purposes. He did NOTHING to look for her, giving the thief a long time to get away. (It took three years to return her to her proper place.)

Here's the point: you have to decide if you will be like today's museum curator who uses his power to carefully protect the Mona Lisa, or if you will be the careless guard who allowed her to be stolen in 1911.

You deserve special protection and care. Modesty is a power that gives you the ability to have yourself properly and safely viewed. (It's not the only way we protect ourselves, and even then we sometimes have to tell someone older and wiser if someone doesn't respect our boundaries for our body.

Remember what I wrote about not keeping "bad secrets" in the introduction? If someone is disrespectful of your body, you should tell someone!)

Do you know who is in charge of that special care? **YOU!** I bet your mom and dad are doing a good job of it or this book wouldn't be in your hand right now, but ultimately it will be **YOU** who is put in charge of the art that is **YOU!**

BUT I do think that modesty gets a bum rap these days. For example, recently a school told girls not to wear form-fitting yoga pants. I think that's a perfectly reasonable dress code for school, but some people get all worked up about the "rights" a girl has to wear yoga pants to school and they say that people who teach modesty are "shaming" girls from showing their bodies. I look at it differently. I think we have the "right" and "responsibility" to present ourselves appropriately in all situations. Some yoga pants may be appropriate in the gym, but in an academic setting I want to wear clothes that allow my brain to be the main event! Not my body. In order for that to happen, I need to wear clothing appropriate—or created for—learning, not stretching. This is where we need to understand the importance and power of modesty.

{
Let me share a little bit more about this power of modesty and why it's a wise choice. Let's go to an ART SHOW!
}

The Art Show

[What we wear becomes sin when it says "look at me" instead of "look at God."]

ZACHARY DONALDSON LOOKED AT ME! And I think I know why. You know that skirt my Aunt Janet made me?

...it had to be the skirt!

The one that goes past my knees and is the longest skirt you've ever seen in your entire life? Mom said I HAD to wear it today! (Aunt Janet and Uncle Andy are arriving from Lancaster for a visit today.) Anyway, back to ZACHARY DONALDSON! In the bathroom Laney Douglas looked at me with disdain and I just COULD NOT wear that skirt like that all day. Danika McAllister to the rescue. She taught me how to roll the waist of my skirt to make it shorter. And make it shorter I did. WAY SHORTER. (The kind of short I would make it if my mom weren't a prude.) And just when I walked out of the bathroom with Danika, there was ZACHARY DONALDSON looking at me. Really, truly looking at me. It had to be the skirt! —Kate (DONALDSON?)

I don't think most girls think that hard about what they wear. Very few of us go to the mall saying, "Let me find something really immodest to wear!" More likely we think, "Chillax! It's just fashion!"

Is it *just* fashion?

I'd like to push you . . . stretch you . . . challenge you. I'll do it all with just one word. Are you ready? Once I discovered this Hebrew word in the Bible, it changed my thinking about how I present myself. Will you stick with me through this? This is the hard part of the book, so brace yourself. Here we go!

I'd like to talk to you about the word *sin*.

What? I thought we were talking about fashion!

Oh, we are. Focus with me now. Remember, I used the word *sin* at the beginning of the book but then softened things up a bit so you knew that fashion isn't sinful.

But sometimes how we use it and approach it can be. Let me show you what I have learned from God's Word.

> How would you define SIN? Take a moment and really think about it.

Let's see how your thinking lines up with the Bible. Of course, it was originally written in the Hebrew and Greek languages. To really understand the word *sin*, we need to go back to the Hebrew Old Testament.

The Hebrew culture revolved around war, so some of the Hebrew words are archery terms. The main Old Testament Hebrew root word for sin is *chatta* (or *hatta*). To pronounce that you kind of spit out a hard "h" sound and add "atta"! Try it.

[ch-atta!]

It most literally translates **"to miss the mark."**

Picture an archer's target. What do you most desire to hit? The bull's-eye! That's the "mark." The intended purpose of aiming your arrow is to hit that prized center mark.

Spiritually, the bull's-eye is anything God intends for you and me. For example, if kindness is God's purpose (and it is), then we "miss the mark" when we are mean girls or frenemies. See?

Of course, in our human minds, when we see someone being a bully, we think: "sinner!"

HIT THE BULL'S-EYE!

But God is much more loving than that! He isn't up there saying, "Bad! Bad girl! You really messed up! That was mean." He is up there saying, "Oh, My sweet masterpiece, you missed the mark! That's not how I designed you to act." And because of His love, He offers us forgiveness. Isn't that amazing? God loves us enough to FORGIVE us, and to let us try again! His standards are demanding. The bull's-eye is small, but His response to sin is packed with far more love than our handed-down definitions.

Let's look at this word, chatta, a little more closely. It's easy to see sin when we see someone miss the target altogether. Murder is a good example.

Can you think of some other sins where the entire target is missed? Add a few to our target above, placing these "big nasties" off of the target.

Did you write things like "lying" or "cheating" or "stealing"? Okay. You're getting it.

Now, you and I both know that sin doesn't have to be this "big" to still be sin. Look at all that space on the target between actually missing the target at all and skillfully hitting the bull's-eye. The meaning of *chatta* doesn't say we "missed the target." It says we "missed the mark"—the dead center of the target . . . the bull's-eye. That's the mark! You can actually hit the target without hitting the bull's-eye, can't you?

We often don't even recognize these "little" sins in our life. Sometimes we just get caught up in the motion of everything around us, and instead of trying to reflect God's holiness, we act like the world around us. Without willfully defying God, we sin. Can you think of some ways that we sometimes miss the bull's-eye but not the target altogether? Gossip sure is a great example of this kind of sin, isn't it? I really don't like gossip, and yet sometimes I'm confronted with the fact that by hanging around it, I've condoned it. Worse yet, I sometimes stick in a few jabs myself.

Add a few of your own "little sins" to the target, placing them on the target but not in the bull's-eye.

GOD'S BEST

GOSSIP

Pssstttt . . . and then she said · · ·

Now I don't want you to think that God has "levels" of sin and that some of it is okay. It all separates us from Him. It's all sin. I'm just trying

to show you how very specific God's Word is. You can think you are "pretty close" to God's intended purpose for you and still miss the mark. It's still sin.

God's target would probably look like this.

I'm wondering, did you include immodesty on any of your other targets? I placed it here on this one so it would stick out. (You knew that was coming, didn't you?) Can you be living what appears to be a sort of clean life but still miss the mark? Still be sinning? I think you can.

You see, sin isn't just the bad things we do; it's also failing to do the good things. God designed you for good. To be kind and love others and worship Him. And there's one good thing that's more important than all the others.

Time for your power verse.

. . . .

Secret #5 Power Verse

"So, whether you eat or drink, or whatever you do, do all to the glory of God." (1 Corinthians 10:31)

. . . .

You were created to glorify God.
Glorify is just a big word that means to **make Him known or visible.** Kind of like the way the **moon** makes the **sun visible** every night. The moon has no light of its own, but **it shows off the beauty of the sun** every night! In that way, the moon makes the sun known **even in the darkness of night.** Glorifying God is like that. **We make God known even when He can't be seen.**

No other purpose is greater than making sure people know and see God in you. And this verse says that anything you do should make people see Him. That includes what you eat, what you drink . . . and what you wear! You were made to cause people to look at God.

The reason immodesty is sin is not because of how short a skirt is or how tight a shirt is. The primary sin of immodesty is that we're saying "look at me" instead of "look at God!"

> 🌸 Secret #5: What we wear becomes sin when it says "look at me" instead of "look at God."

hat do I mean by that? Well, a lot of times when we reach for a super blingy shirt or an unusually short skirt, it's because we want to say, "Hey, world! Here I am!" There can be a lot of pride and self-focus in the way that we dress. (Of course, sometimes we just really like the dazzly T-shirt and our heart isn't meaning to be the center of attention, and sometimes that is okay.) But if our intention is to say "look at me," it's not okay. It's not appropriate. Because our entire life is meant to glorify God and to say "look at God!"

I really like fashion, but if I dress super crazy when I teach on stage at True Girl, you might have a hard time hearing the Bible verses I'm using to teach you. I don't want the way that I dress to distract from the good work I'm doing to help you see God. Does that make some sense? We say "look at God" best by the good things we do and the gentleness, kindness, and helpfulness we wear on the inside! Remember this power verse from our last chapter?

"*I want women to be modest in their appearance. They should wear decent and appropriate clothing and not draw attention to themselves by the way they fix their hair or by wearing gold or pearls or expensive clothes.* **For women who claim to be devoted to God should make themselves attractive by the good things they do.**"
(*1 Timothy 2:9–10* NLT)

It's the good things we do that should make us attractive, not the awesome clothes we buy! For that reason, when I'm buying clothes—and I really like shopping and fashion—I'm careful to ask myself, "Will this distract people from seeing God in me? Does it say 'look at Dannah' or does it allow my life to say 'look at God'?"

LOOK AT GOD!

Here's another verse that I need to share with you!

> "So whoever knows the
> right thing to do and fails to do it,
> for him it is sin." (James 4:17)

rom this day forward, you know the right thing to do. You know that
God wants you to dress carefully and modestly so that nothing you wear
distracts people from seeing the good things you do so that they can see Jesus in
you. Now that you know this: if you fail to do it, it is sin.

Remember, the bull's-eye represents God's intended purpose for your life. His
intended purpose for your beauty is to glorify Him—that is, to help people see
Him. When we dress modestly so that nothing distracts from the good works
we do, people can see God's fingerprint in our internal beauty! When we dress
carelessly so that our bodies are the primary focus, people get distracted and can't
see inside of us to see God. So does all this talk about sin sound harsh? Well,
stick with me, because sin is not the most important word in the Bible, and it's
not the most important word in this book. That's coming up in the next chapter.

THE "Truth OR Bare" Fashion Tests!

FASHION CHALLENGE!

How do you know if an outfit is modest or not?
Well, there's no sure way, but we do have some
ideas. Try these "Truth or Bare" Fashion Tests!
I developed them with my team. We didn't want
them to be a set of legalistic rules. Instead, we
wanted to create something that would help you
start the thinking process and let your heart be
molded into modesty. These may work for you, or
you may want to develop your own tests.

Raise & Praise

"AM I SHOWING TOO MUCH BELLY?"

Stand and pretend you are totally going for it in worship, lifting your hands in the air with your arms fully extended. Is this exposing any belly skin? Even if you don't raise your hands to worship, just think of all the things you do every day that cause you to lift them.

TEST

1

SOLUTION: Go for layers and put a longer shirt under a shorter one. Our Secret Weapon: a ribbed T-shirt or tank from the boys' or men's department. They're nice and long and stay tucked in under a cool, trendy shirt. No problem here since she's got one under her button-down!

I See London, I See France

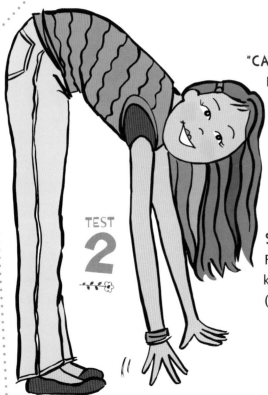

TEST 2

"CAN YOU SEE MY UNDERPANTS?"

Bend over and check yourself out in the mirror. (You got it . . . the back view!) Can you see a distinct outline of your panties through your pants, skirt, or shorts? This can happen if your pants are too tight or your undies are too bright!

SOLUTION: Trash your tight pants. For lighter colored pants and skirts, keep a few pairs of "granny panties" (plain white or beige ones) on hand for a safe look.

Mirror Image

"HOW SHORT IS TOO SHORT?"

When you buy either shorts or a skirt, try this test. Sit "criss-cross applesauce" in front of a full-length mirror. What do you see? If you see too much thigh or your panties, guess what? So can everyone else.

TEST 3

SOLUTION: Today's skirts are about extremes. Go for extremely long or extremely full . . . but pass on extremely short. As far as shorts go, longer ones can be hard to find, but keep looking!

The Plumber's Test

"ARE MY PANTS JUST TOO LOW?"
It ain't cute on the plumber, and it ain't cute on girls either. The terrible . . . the awful . . . crack view! Sit cross-legged on the floor. Bend forward as if you're about to devour a great magazine. Now, reach behind you and get a feel of what might be the featured view if your jeans are too low. (Or ask a girlfriend to check it out!)

SOLUTION: Time to reach for that Secret Weapon again: a guy's tank or T-shirt. And always be willing to consider that some low riders are just too low. Find a pair that won't cause viewers to blush.

Stand In The Gap

"TELL ME NOW . . . IS MY SHIRT TOO TIGHT?"
When wearing a button-down shirt, stand sideways and look in the mirror. Is the space between the buttons gaping open, even just a little bit? If it's pulling enough to cause a gap, you're in danger of exposing way too much and in danger of losing a button!

SOLUTION: It's a no-brainer. Too-tight shirts are a totally bad idea if you want to dress modestly. It's not JUST about how much of your beautiful epidermis is showing, but how much of your shape is showing! Try buying a size or two larger. (If that bugs you, cut out the tag when you get home.) Or try a shirt under the button-down, and leave the shirt unbuttoned for a layered look.

TEST

5

Palm Pilot

TEST 6

"IS MY SHIRT TOO LOW?"

How do you know if your shirt is too low? Well, take your hand and hook your thumb onto that little shelf under your neck. (That's your collarbone. Feel around. You'll find it.) Now, lay your palm nice and flat on your chest so the pinkie is about 5-6 inches under the thumb. Is there any skin showing below your pinkie? If so, you really need to think about this shirt.

SOLUTION: Guess what? Our Secret Weapon works for low shirts as well as short shirts! You can also try a trendy layering technique by putting a button-down under a polo or rugby shirt that plunges too low.

THE **SECRET** Weapon

Grab a few of these in the boys' or men's department. **Simple tank T's.** They're great wardrobe lifesavers. Why the men's department? Because they make men's shirts nice and long and you'll have lots to tuck into your pants or keep long for the layered look.

Keep your eyes open. I find tanks of varying colors that are nice and long at some of my favorite stores just for girls! Once you have a collection, you'll always have a great modest and trendy fashion solution on hand!

The Bottom line

[If you love God, you will obey Him in the way you dress.]

. . . protecting his "wittle girl."

Is it my fault I can play ball better than most boys? No! But my dad is so obsessed with what I wear when I play with them, that he can't even see my mad skills. Grrrrrrr! Today before he would drive me to practice, he made me go back to my room and change. TWICE. He said my pants were too tight. Too tight for what, running around the bases? Sitting on the bench to wait my turn? Knocking the ball outta the park? Dad says he's just protecting his "wittle girl." Oh brother! I feel half crazy because I don't want to need protecting.

On the other hand, when I thought about it I really do trust my dad even though I don't understand what he's thinking! Yeah, I love him. So, I'll stick with sweatpants when I play ball with the boys. -Toni

Do you find all this modesty stuff hard to swallow? Have I ruffled your feathers? Would you rather not know these simple truths I've taught you because it means you have to either reject or embrace them? I understand. They can be a pain in the neck, and some people get so uptight about fashion. I assure you that if I saw you looking absolutely adorable in something trendy, I would say "You look adorbs!" I like fashion, but I love Jesus! And I want to make sure my life shines for Him. So, I have embraced the Bible's teaching on beauty and fashion. **AND MODESTY!**

I remember a time in sixth grade when my dad didn't like my shoes. **My shoes!** My Nana gave me those shoes when she didn't want to wear them anymore. They were royal blue fabric heels. They were better for dancing than for doing math, but my dad said they were "boy catcher" shoes. (He had a way of being extreme sometimes when it came to protecting me.) They said, "Here I am! Look at me!" They did not say, "Look at God!"

I was dressed for school and running to catch my bus when my dad noticed me. He calmly pulled the newspaper away from his face and said, "You need to change your shoes into something sensible before you leave for school."

And then he put his newspaper back up.

"Daaaaddddd! I'll miss the school bus." I whined.

As calmly as he could, my dad simply said, "Then, prepare to walk to school!"

Of course, he didn't really mean it. My school was 20 miles away from my house, but his message was clear: you're changing your shoes one way or another.

I am afraid I didn't act as if I loved my dad that day, and for that I'm sorry. I pouted and stomped out the door in my boring flats. Now I realize that my dad was just protecting me because he **LOVED ME!**

WOW!

Think about it. When your mom and dad put boundaries on the things you do, they are really saying, "I love you."

💜 **WHEN** they don't let you play in the street when you're a toddler, it's because they love you and don't want you to get hit by a car.

💜 **WHEN** they don't let you eat ice cream before you eat veggies, it's because they love you and don't want your body to be addicted to sugar.

💜 **WHEN** they don't let you go to a movie that's not okay, it's because they love you and don't want you to have images in your head that you can't get out.

💜 **WHEN** they don't let you wear a super short skirt to school, it's because they love you and want people to see the brains and beauty **INSIDE** of you and not to get stuck on the outside stuff.

OK now that we have established that rules mean your parents love you, let's imagine every time your mom or dad says "no" you can actually hear them saying, "I love you!" (Of course, you're going to have to listen real hard to hear that, I'm sure. But play along!)

What do you say when someone you love says, "I love you"?

You say, "I love you" back!

How do you say that when the way they say "I love you" is putting boundaries on your behavior? You obey them! And you do it with a good heart!

Let me be honest with you. If you don't like what you're reading in this book or are planning to ignore it, you probably don't have a modesty problem. *You have a love problem.*

You see, sin is not the most important word in the Bible. **LOVE** is.

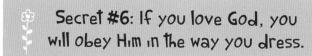

🌸 Secret #6: If you love God, you
will obey Him in the way you dress.

You see, when you truly love God, you obey Him. His guidelines for living may still be hard to swallow, but you still follow them because you realize it's about *loving Him.*

Secret #6 Power Verse

*"Whoever has my commandments and keeps them,
he it is who loves me. And he who loves me
will be loved by my Father, and I will love him
and manifest myself to him."* (John 14:21)

I f you are struggling to obey God in the area of modesty, maybe it's just because you and I can be really stubborn sometimes when it comes to obeying God. But maybe it's because you do not really know Him and His deep love for you. It's easy to know about God and His Son. Lots of people do. But few actually, really intimately know Him. And when you do truly know Him, you can't help but love Him.

DO YOU LOVE HIM? ♥ HE SURE LOVES YOU!

How do I know? Because the way He has responded to your sin and mine is so radically, crazy full of love. It's normal to get in trouble when you do something wrong. Once I talked back to my dad and got grounded for a week. No parties. No TV. No friends. No soccer practice. Nothing! I was in my room doing homework or doing chores when I wasn't at school. I deserved that punishment. It was normal for my mom and dad to react that way. And in that case, normal was good.

But God isn't normal. And He doesn't treat us normally either. He doesn't treat us the way we *deserve* to be treated! Psalm 103:9–10 says, "He never bears a grudge, nor remains angry forever. He has not punished us as we deserve for all our sins" (TLB).

Don't get me wrong. God handed out a punishment for your sins.

🦋 That lie you told . . .

🦋 The mean thing you said to a classmate . . .

🦋 The sass you gave your mom last week . . .

Those sins did not go unpunished.

But you weren't the one who had to take the punishment. And the punishment was real, real harsh! Romans 6:23 says the punishment for sin is *death*!

[BUT!]

Our God is not normal. He loves like **CRAZY!!** Romans 6:23 in all of its glory reads: "The wages of sin is death, but the free gift of God is eternal life in Christ Jesus our Lord"! So if you didn't have to pay the penalty for your sin, who did? Jesus did! Isaiah 53 says God put

on Him all the weight of our sin. Jesus paid it all. He went to the cross carrying every one of our sins upon His back—our lying, our meanness, our disobedience—and He paid it all for you and for me **BECAUSE HE LOVES US!** He wanted to give us the free gift of forgiveness and eternal life.

The only thing we have to do is accept His free gift, and when we do, it's kind of like being adopted into this family. Because we become a part of the family of God.

I adopted my daughter Autumn when she was 13 years old. It was one of the best days of my life. You know, when we adopted her, she had to go in front of a judge and testify that she *wanted* to be adopted. Coming into God's family is a little like that. You have to **CHOOSE IT**. I'm wondering if you've ever done that? Do you

remember a time when you did?

If you don't, put this book down and talk to your mom right now and ask her! (Come back after you and her have a good talk.)

If you do, keep reading!

Make no mistake. It is God who desires for you to dress modestly and reveal your inner beauty by protecting you with modesty. When we love Him, this comes a tad more naturally. Don't try to just dress how God wants you to dress unless you first have been adopted into His family and entered into His LOVE!

If Jesus were to write you a love note, I think this might be what it would say. I got the truths in most of the sentences in this love note from verses in the Bible. I just rewrote them directly to you.

My Precious Masterpiece,

Have the bad-hair days and expensive brand-name jeans your mom won't buy you gotten the worst of you? Oh, if only you could see how brilliant a masterpiece you are.

I couldn't wait for you to arrive. You! Yes, you! I've anticipated your presence on My earth before it was even created.

Like a master embroiderer sits at his loom painstakingly interweaving each unique strand, I knit you together piece by piece with intention and precision. You are one of the unique expressions of My own glory. I chose the color of your hair from the earth and the color of your eyes from the beauty of My creation. I even placed My thumb there on your nose, marking it with My fingerprint.

After you were made in secret, I revealed you to this world, with still the most profound parts of your beauty waiting to be crafted. Still, I am creating you in secret, My masterpiece.

Though the full secrets of your beauty are unknown to the world, I see. And I am enthralled by your beauty.

Oh, how I love you.

There have been only a few places on earth that I have been willing to fill with My own radiant glory—the tabernacle, the old temple . . . and you! That's how precious your body is to Me.

Will you honor Me with it?

Will you love Me back?

Your Master Craftsman, Jesus*

*This letter from Jesus is written using Ephesians 1:4–7;
Psalm 139:13–16; Psalm 45:11–14; 1 Corinthians 6:19–20.

DO YOU LOVE HIM?

"Or do you not know that your body is a
temple of the Holy Spirit within you,
whom you have from God? You are not your own,
for you were bought with a price.
So glorify God in your body."
(1 Corinthians 6:19–20)

Finding True Beauty

[The source of true beauty is a love relationship with Jesus!]

...maybe even ... pretty!

Dear God, I've been writing in this journal a whole lot and noticed something. Sometimes I write to You. Sometimes I just write. Without a doubt the times I write to You, I feel better. I mean, it's cool to write about Zachary Donaldson appearances and who got picked first in gym class, but where does it get me? Usually, just more frustrated. But when I write to You, I feel peaceful. Happy. Maybe even ... pretty! So, I dedicate this diary to talking to You! From this day to forever! —Danika

I can't let you go without telling you how to get true beauty! Just where does it really come from? I mean, we know it's not something you can buy at the mall. Wouldn't it be easier if there were a True Beauty Mall? Can you imagine the beautiful inner shoes for your feet to carry the love of Jesus to other people that could be found at Pay-It-Forward Shoes? And, oh, the jewels for your heart like earrings of grace, and chokers of self-control, and bracelets of joy to be found at Clara's Inner Beauty Jewelry Boutique? And the garments that get us geared up to do good works at Justice Good Deeds Duds? (Did you see what I did there? I tried to use the names of famous name brands with a twist. I crack myself up!)

WHAT?!

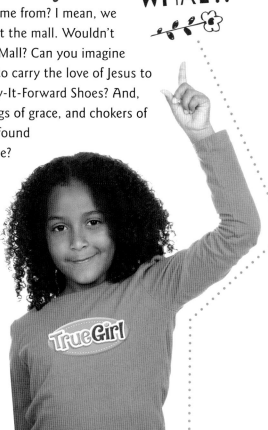

Okay, there is no True Beauty Mall.

So, I'm going to tell you where to go to get true beauty. But first, let's review the six secrets we learned in the first six chapters of this book. (By the way, good job making it this far. This is really a self-help book and lots of girls aren't ready for them until high school, but I'm proud of you for devouring this one!)

[REVIEW OF TRUE BEAUTY SECRETS!]

1. You are a masterpiece created by God.

2. True beauty doesn't come from what's on the outside.

3. True beauty is not about how you look. It's about how you see.

4. God wants nothing we wear to distract people from seeing our true beauty.

5. What we wear becomes sin when it says "look at me" instead of "look at God."

6. If you love God, you will obey Him in the way you dress.

Now, it's time for **Secret #7**, which tells us where to get true beauty. The fact is, you *can* "get" it somewhere.

I got it and when I did, I didn't hate what I saw when I looked in the mirror. And trust me, I used to hate it so much that I would **not** look in the mirror. This started in my tweens and lasted all the way through my college years. I actually learned how to put mascara on without looking in the mirror because I disliked what I saw there so very much . . . until I found the Source of true beauty. Now I actually like what I see. It's not like I look in the mirror and say, "Wow, girl! You are one gorgeous chick!" No, I just kind of look in the mirror and know I'm a masterpiece created by God and think one very simple thought: "What He made is good." Oh, it gives me butterflies in my tummy right now as I write this and think of you finding that.

I've been helping girls find it ever since I started True Girl in 2003, using a different name. That's a lot of years ago. (You weren't even born yet!) So I really love helping girls experience God and His Presence.

About 450,000 girls and moms have attended one of my live True Girl events, where I teach them how to find the Source of true beauty. God is bringing to my mind some girls who found it.

Here is what girls have experienced when they use this last secret
• FAITHFULLY

They begin to think insanely GREAT things about being a masterpiece created by God, and I DO want *you* to think these things!

One girl in Canada who always used bulky, oversized clothes to cover herself up and hide her body began to think that she was actually quite beautiful. She began working out and wearing clothes that were modest but never failed to be super cute. *She began to think that she was a masterpiece created by God.* (DO that!)

One girl in Pittsburgh, Pennsylvania, who had to have a lot of corrective surgeries on her teeth and jaws began to see all those painful experiences as a way God was giving her more than just beautiful teeth. She began to think He was giving her "heart" surgery so she could learn patience, perseverance, and courage. *She began to think that God had purpose in her physical suffering.* (DO that!)

One girl in Jarabacoa, Dominican Republic, who disliked herself so badly that she was doing terrible things to physically change her body, stopped hurting herself. She began to think that God made her right after all and started to have contentment and gratitude for how she was created. *She began to think she should teach other girls that they were just right the way they were created, too.* (DO that!)

One girl in California who dressed in super-tight clothes and super-short shorts and super-low-cut shirts threw them all away one day. She asked her mom to take her to the Goodwill store to buy "new" vintagey clothes because she wanted to dress modestly. No one told her to do that. *She began to think she could choose to obey God.* **(DO that!)**

Here's the thing: the secret I'm about to teach you **works**.

It's been proven over and over again that what I'm about to tell you to do will make you feel better about yourself. In fact, I've never heard from one girl or woman who did what I'm going to ask of you who didn't feel better about herself after the time was up. (It's gonna take a bit to let it all sink in.)

It's important to return to something I said before: feelings aren't facts. But when we base what we feel on facts and feel better about something because it's truth, it's good! It's good to have good feelings because you have found truthful facts to live by.

Using God's standard and His way of finding true beauty to make you feel better about yourself is like drinking refreshing water from a huge fire hose. You'll never even be able to drink all of what He has to give you.

IT'S NOT ALWAYS EASY!

I know that this secret—more than all the others—can make you feel confident and aaamazing, **IF YOU DO WHAT I ASK OF YOU!**

There's the rub! This isn't going to come easy. It's not for the girl who can't roll up her sleeves and do a little hard stuff. I have found that I have to be **FAITHFUL** to get into God's Word and do a lot of hard stuff in order to feel His presence. What kind of hard stuff? Like getting up early to read the Bible. Or staying up late. Or saying "no" when a friend wants to hang out because I know I need to spend some time praying. It's not always easy. But it's always rewarding. It makes me feel more confident. And the sense of God's presence is aaamazing!.

Do you want to feel confident and aaamazing?

Read on!

Take a look at this power verse, which we used earlier in the book.

"Your beauty should not come from outward adornment, such as elaborate hairstyles and the wearing of gold jewelry or fine clothes. Rather, it should be that of your inner self, the unfading beauty of a gentle and quiet spirit, which is of great worth in God's sight." (1 Peter 3:3–4 NIV)

When do you get a gentle and quiet spirit? You get it when your inner self is made beautiful by a love relationship with Jesus.

Secret #7: The source of true beauty is a love relationship with Jesus!

What 1 Peter 3:3–4 is really challenging is this: "Do you spend more time in front of the mirror making yourself externally beautiful, or do you spend more time developing your inner beauty through quiet communion with God?"

. . . .

Secret #7 Power Verse
"You shall love the LORD your God with all your heart and with all your soul and with all your might."
(Deuteronomy 6:5)

. . . .

It takes **STRENGTH** to love God. All of our STRENGTH! That means you put effort into it, and that's what I'd like to encourage you to do. I'd like to ask you to take my **True Girl Beauty Challenge**. Here's how it works:

Challenge yourself each day to spend a little more time with God than you spend working on your external self. If your morning beauty routine is fifteen minutes, try for twenty minutes of time alone with God. Although I don't want you to get caught up in watching the clock, I know that pushing yourself in this area of discipline will change you immensely. Let me say this one more time: it's not about watching the clock but taking care to be more concerned with grooming your heart than your face. Make sense?

I want you to do this for the next seven weeks, for five out of seven days a week. **WHOA!** That sounds like a big investment of time, doesn't it? Well, I've been doing it for twenty-three **YEARS!** Do you know what's happened? I've changed from a girl who disliked what I saw in the mirror so much that I would not look in it to a woman who looks in the mirror and thinks, "I'm a masterpiece created by God!"

Working on my internal beauty has helped me to accept my external beauty. And I like spending time increasing my love relationship with Jesus so much that I keep doing it year after year, month after month, day after day. You might like it that much, too. But I'm only asking you to do it for **SEVEN WEEKS!** Why seven weeks? Because they say it takes forty days to develop a habit, and I want spending time in God's presence to become a habit for you.

A lot of people will say I'm crazy for asking you. (*That's not what God says.* He says we should start EVERY DAY with prayer. That's Psalm 119:147.)

Some people will say you are too young. (*That is not what God says.* He says "Don't let anyone look down on you because you are young, but set an example for the believers in speech, in conduct, in love, in faith and in purity." That's 1 Timothy 4:12 NIV.)

Some people will say there are better things to do with your time. No way! There's no better use of your time than spending it on Jesus! In fact, it says He's supposed to be the FIRST thing that we spend time on (Matthew 6:33). You can do this. I would not be asking this big thing from you if I didn't believe that you could do it.

B Ask your mom to join you in the challenge. It helps a lot to have someone doing it with you. You can agree to the challenge by signing the True Girl Beauty Challenge on the next page. After you both sign it, tear it out and tape it to your bathroom mirror.

C Every day, before you officially start your day, spend time reading God's Word and praying on your own. Once a week, check in with your mom.

A really great tool to use during these seven weeks is the *True Girl Mom-Daughter Devos with Coloring Experience.* I wrote it just for this **True Girl Beauty Challenge.** It has devotions written for you to use five days a week, and the last one of the week is a coloring experience for you and your mom. You can color while you talk about the lessons you've learned.

Of course, you can do this without the *True Girl Mom-Daughter Devos with Coloring Experience* by using your own devotional tools or even just the Bible and a journal.

Or, you could go to mytruegirl.com and sign up for my **FREE Ten-Day True Girl Beauty Challenge.** You'll find it on the home page. These ten devotions on true beauty would get you started, so the first two weeks would be all ready to go!

No matter how you approach it, every day I want you to ask yourself the question:

$$\left\{ \begin{array}{c} \text{"Today, did I spend more} \\ \text{time in God's Word or} \\ \text{in front of this mirror?"} \end{array} \right\}$$

Are you ready to dive in?
If so, **Sign** the True Girl Beauty Challenge. And **dive in!**

TrueGirl

BEAUTY CHALLENGE:

{ "Today, did I spend more time in God's Word or in front of this mirror?" }

"Your beauty should not come from outward adornment, such as elaborate hairstyles and the wearing of gold jewelry or fine clothes. Rather, it should be that of your inner self, the unfading beauty of a gentle and quiet spirit, which is of great worth in God's sight." (I Peter 3:3–4 NIV)

We, _____ and

_____, will attempt to

spend_____ and_____minutes a day in quiet

prayer and Bible reading during the next seven weeks.

We commit to do this for five out of every seven days.

Signed:_____

Date: _____

Signed:_____

Date: _____

The True Girl Beauty Challenge is a creation of Dannah Gresh, as published in *True Girl: Discover the Secrets of True Beauty* by Moody Publishers. To learn more, go to mytruegirl.com.

APPENDIX

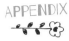

The Secrets of True Beauty for Every True Girl

(And the power verses you need!)

1 You are a masterpiece created by God. "I praise you, for I am fearfully and wonderfully made. Wonderful are your works; my soul knows it very well. My frame was not hidden from you, when I was being made in secret, intricately woven . . ." Psalm 139:14–15

2 True beauty doesn't come from what's on the outside. "Your beauty should not come from outward adornment, such as elaborate hairstyles and the wearing of gold jewelry or fine clothes." 1 Peter 3:3 (NIV)

3 True beauty is not about how you look. It's about how you see. "Be beautiful inside, in your hearts, with the lasting charm of a gentle and quiet spirit that is so precious to God." 1 Peter 3:4 (TLB)

4 God wants nothing we wear to distract people from seeing our true beauty. "I want women to be modest in their appearance. They should wear decent and appropriate clothing and not draw attention to themselves by the way they fix their hair or by wearing gold or pearls or expensive clothes. For women who claim to be devoted to God should make themselves attractive by the good things they do." 1 Timothy 2:9–10 (NLT)

5 What we wear becomes sin when it says "look at me" instead of "look at God." "So whoever knows the right thing to do and fails to do it, for him it is sin." James 4:17

6 If you love God, you will obey Him in the way you dress. "Whoever has my commandments and keeps them, he it is who loves me. And he who loves me will be loved by my Father, and I will love him and manifest myself to him." John 14:21

7 The source of true beauty is a love relationship with Jesus! "You shall love the LORD your God with all your heart and with all your soul and with all your might." Deuteronomy 6:5

NOTES

1. "secret," definition #11, http://www.dictionary.com/browse/secret.

2. Girls aged 8–12 spend about $500 million per year on beauty products alone! Deborah Swaney, "Fast Times: When did 7 become the new 16?" *Family Circle*, November 29, 2008, 48.

3. According to one Harvard study, two-thirds of underweight twelve-year-olds considered themselves fat, 80% of ten year olds have been on a diet, and 34% cut back on their eating without telling mom. *Good Housekeeping*, August 1, 2006.

4. This thought about being a coward or having courage is from the introduction in C. S. Lewis's *Mere Christianity*. It's not an original thought.

5. "counterfeit," definition #3, http://www.dictionary.com/browse/counterfeit.

6. This text and some other material was adapted from text originally published in my book *Secret Keeper: The Delicate Power of Modesty* (Chicago: Moody, 2002).

7. "curator," definition #1, http://www.dictionary.com/browse/curator.

This book
gets even
better when
you use its
companion!

TAKE THE

True Girl Beauty Challenge!

I dare you to spend the next 35 days spending more time in God's presence than you do brushing your teeth, styling your hair, and getting dressed in the morning. It's that easy. A companion to *True Girl*, these 35 days of mother/daughter devos with weekly coloring experiences will help you get more excited about having a beautiful heart rather than a beautiful face!

Some people will say I'm crazy for asking you to take on this challenge, but God says we should start every day with prayer. Some will say you're too young, but God says not to let anyone look down on you because you are young. So rise up to this challenge! It'll help you find the true beauty within you.

For other books, blogs, events and more by
Dannah Gresh visit, MyTrueGirl.com

MOODY
Publishers®

From the Word to Life®

*For more resources and events
for tween girls, go to*

MYTRUEGIRL.COM

IMAGE CREDITS